INDEX

STAMP
COLLECTING

by IAN F. FINLAY, M.A.

Publishers : Wills & Hepworth Ltd. Loughborough
First published 1969   ©   *Printed in England*

The days before adhesive stamps

The General Letter Office (the forerunner of the present General Post Office) was established in 1660 during the reign of Charles II. Much of the mail was carried by Post Boys, some of whom walked while others rode on horseback. Later, in the eighteenth century, the mail was carried by stage coach.

In those days before postage stamps, a letter was put in an envelope (a 'pre-stamp cover') which was addressed and possibly sealed with sealing wax. When the letter was delivered, the person to whom it was addressed had to pay a delivery charge based, amongst other things, on the distance it had been carried. He could, in fact, have refused to pay the charge, and there would have been nothing anyone could do about it. Until 1840 this system was used in most parts of the world, although there were various attempts to improve it by prepayment of the delivery charge.

In the lower illustration is a 'pre-stamp' cover – an envelope used in November, 1836, to enclose a letter sent across the Netherlands. There are only a date and place name on it – no postage stamp.

0 7214 0235 6

The first adhesive stamp

On May 6th, 1840, adhesive stamps for the prepayment of postage were on sale for the first time in England, and, in fact, for the first time anywhere in the world. This idea was developed largely by Sir Rowland Hill, and was the beginning of postage stamps as we know them. After much research into postage costs and administration, he proved that there was no benefit in charging according to the distance over which a letter was carried. For example, the cost of conveying a letter from London to Edinburgh (for which $1/4\frac{1}{2}$d. had been charged) was then only 1/36th part of a penny. His scheme for a prepaid postage charge of one penny – regardless of distance – was introduced after much hostile Government and official opposition.

The first stamp – the 'Penny Black' – was a black stamp with a portrait of Queen Victoria, and with the words 'Postage' and 'One Penny', and various check letters in the bottom corners. Since it was the world's first stamp, there was no need to put the name of the issuing country on it. This omission of the name of the country, and the inclusion of the sovereign's head, have remained characteristic features of the stamps of Great Britain ever since.

Above: Sir Rowland Hill.
Below: 1966 Umm Al Qiwain stamp illustrating the 'Penny Black'.

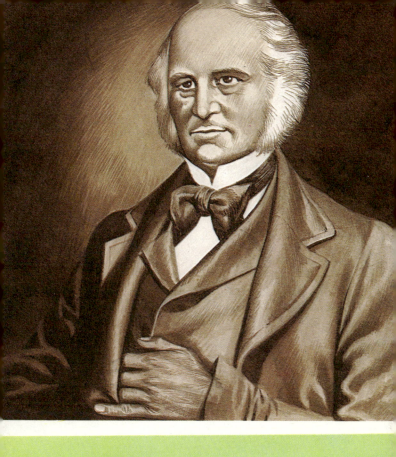

POSTAGE

CENTENARY STAMP EXHIBITION, CAIRO 1966

G ONE PENNY B

POSTAGE

3 NP

UMM AL QIWAIN

Early postage stamps

For a while, Great Britain was the only country to have stamps. However, it was realised that the idea was a good one, and other countries soon began to introduce their own postage stamps. The first was Brazil and then parts of Switzerland in 1843. The United States followed in 1847 and Belgium, France and Bavaria in 1849. Reproductions of most of these early stamps were included in the special set prepared by Umm Al Qiwain for the 1966 stamp exhibition in Cairo, and some are illustrated opposite. The influence of the 'Penny Black' on their design is obvious.

All early stamps were modelled on the coins of the countries issuing them; that is to say, they showed either the head of the sovereign or the arms of the country. They may in some ways appear dull to us, but they were really masterpieces of the engraver's art and were very much better designed than some of the stamps issued later.

1966 Umm Al Qiwain stamps illustrating early postage stamps.

Stamps become more interesting

Although early stamps were based on coins for their designs, it was not long before most countries conceived the idea of illustrating various other things on them, such as historical events, views of their countries, famous men, and industrial or agricultural products. These were the beginnings of the trend towards pictorial, or 'thematic' stamps. Thematic stamps are now the rule rather than the exception, and the stamp album has become a very interesting, colourful and educational object.

Our illustrations of early pictorials come from the United States (1898), Cuba (1898), Spain (1905), Bosnia and Herzogovina (1906), Rumania (1906), Chile (1910), while the Sudan stamp issued in 1948 shows a reproduction of the famous Arab postman issue of 1898. If we compare them with the stamps on the previous page, the progress in designing will be clear.

Some early pictorial stamps.

 **UNITED STATES (1898)**

 CUBA (1898)

 **SPAIN (1905)**

BOSNIA and HERZOGOVINA (1906)

 **RUMANIA (1906)**

 **CHILE (1910)**

SUDAN (1948)

Ships and boats on stamps

Of all forms of transport, ships and boats of one type or another are probably the oldest. It is, therefore, understandable that it should be possible to trace their history on stamps to a fuller extent than is possible with most other forms of transport. Our illustrations can therefore represent only a very small selection of these interesting stamps.

The San Marino stamp (1963) shows a Greek vessel from the second century B.C., while the Canadian stamp (1949) on the bottom left of page, shows Cabot's ship 'Matthew' which sailed at about the end of the fifteenth century. Moving forward to the nineteenth century, we see a Mississippi riverboat, such as those often described by Mark Twain, and a whaling ship from Norway. The stamp from the Falkland Island Dependencies (1952) shows a modern ship for use in the Antarctic, while that from West Germany (1965) illustrates a modern liner and a nineteenth-century steamship. The remaining stamps show primitive craft from northern Canada (top right), and from the British Solomon Islands in the Pacific (bottom right).

Ships and boats.

SAN MARINO

CANADA

UNITED STATES

NORWAY

**FALKLAND ISLANDS
DEPENDENCIES**

WEST GERMANY

CANADA

BRITISH SOLOMON ISLANDS

Stamps and land transport

All forms of land transport have always been popular subjects for stamps, both among the authorities issuing them and among collectors. Once again, we can illustrate only a selection.

The special delivery stamp from the United States shows a motor cycle dating from 1922, while the next stamp from Great Britain features a number of Minis and an 'E' type Jaguar car. The diamond-shaped stamp from Hungary shows an exciting scene from sidecar racing. The next stamp, also from Hungary, illustrates an articulated trolley-bus in Budapest, while the parcel post stamp from Bulgaria features a motor-cycle combination used for delivery purposes. On the Russian stamp we can see a scene from a cycle race, while the last stamp, again from the United States, was issued as part of a campaign to stop road accidents. It bears the inscription 'enforcement, education, engineering', these being the three most important factors in the prevention of road accidents.

Cycles, motor cycles, cars and road safety.

UNITED STATES

GREAT BRITAIN

HUNGARY

RUSSIA

BULGARIA

UNITED STATES

Airmail stamps

Although the first carrying of mail by air was by means of balloon as early as 1859 in the United States, it was not until the development of the aeroplane by the Wright Brothers, in the early years of this century, that the regular carriage of mail by air began to take place. This had its effects on the stamp world. Special stamps were issued to be used on mail carried by air, and many stamps appeared showing various types of aircraft. Our illustrations show both these effects.

The stamp from San Marino shows the Wright Brothers' aeroplane of 1904, while the Australian stamp, issued in 1954, shows the type of aeroplane used to carry that country's first airmail in July 1914. Our remaining illustrations show a stamp from Chile depicting a flying boat, a Belgian stamp issued in 1963 illustrating a 'Caravelle' jet aircraft, one of the stamps issued by the Netherlands in 1959 to commemorate the fiftieth anniversary of the Royal Dutch Airlines and, finally, an airmail stamp from Hungary, showing an aeroplane flying over the Budapest Opera House.

Old and new aircraft.

SAN MARINO

AUSTRALIA

CHILE

BELGIUM

NETHERLANDS

HUNGARY

Stamps and animals

Almost every living creature has been illustrated on postage stamps, so our selection can only represent a very small part of the 'stamp zoo'.

We begin with three of the strange animals found today only in Australia. They are the kookaburra, the koala bear and the kangaroo. There is a hare on the stamp from Hungary, and a very formidable reptile, the stegosaurus, on a stamp from a set issued by Poland in 1965 and devoted to prehistoric animals. Below it is a stamp from Poland featuring the much more friendly tortoise, and to the left of that a picture of that lovable creature, the giant panda, on a stamp from The People's Republic of China.

At the bottom, on the left, is a stamp from a Rumanian set devoted to local fairy tales. It shows the proverbial wolf in sheep's clothing! To the right of that a gorilla is shown on a stamp from Ruanda-Urundi, a former Belgian territory in Africa. Altogether an interesting and varied collection.

Some animals of the world.

AUSTRALIA

HUNGARY

POLAND

CHINA

RUMANIA

RUANDA-URUNDI

Stamps and food

It is certainly true today that there is hardly any subject or object that has not been portrayed on a postage stamp. Food is perhaps one of the last things you would expect to find illustrated on stamps, but the following examples show that this subject, too, has been very well covered. To see some of these beautiful stamps is almost enough to make your mouth water!

The first two stamps come from Rumania and are from a set issued in 1963 featuring fruits and nuts. Our examples show two luscious apples and a collection of walnuts. The Polish stamp shows a fisherman holding a large fish, obviously one of those which did not get away! The stamp from Czechoslovakia shows a corn cob which looks very inviting. The stamp from Israel shows some of the fine oranges that grow in that country.

The further stamp from Rumania, issued in 1962 in connection with an agricultural project, shows a wheat-sheaf, while that from Norway, issued in 1963 in connection with the Freedom from Hunger campaign, shows a collection of various foodstuffs, including fish, fruit and vegetables. Finally, the stamp from France shows some of the beautiful locally produced china and glass, from which one could eat and drink the attractive food and wines portrayed on the stamps of many other countries.

Foods and eating utensils.

RUMANIA

POLAND

ISRAEL

CZECHOSLOVAKIA

RUMANIA

FRANCE

NORWAY

Stamps and clothes

There are various aspects of clothes that you can study through postage stamps. These include not only the various animals and plants that supply us with the skins and fibres from which we make our clothes, but also the numerous colourful dresses and costumes worn in different parts of the world. Various pieces of textile machinery have also been portrayed on stamps, so that this is another field in which you can gather a comprehensive collection.

Our first stamp, from the Sudan, shows a native weaving on a primitive loom. The Rumanian stamp shows a silk-worm feeding on a mulberry leaf, while the stamp from Ethiopia shows a scene inside a modern textile mill. The next stamp, from the Falkland Islands, illustrates two sheep. The stamp from Montserrat shows a field of sea-island cotton.

The Greek stamp pictures a former member of the Greek royal family wearing a very beautiful and elaborate local costume, while that from the Portuguese territory of Angola in Africa shows two of the local inhabitants in their colourful native costumes. It comes from a set devoted to local types and costumes. Finally, the stamp from Rumania, issued in 1962 in connection with a Sample Fair held in the capital, Bucharest, shows a sewing-machine and various other items used in the home.

Raw materials for making clothes and some national costumes.

SUDAN

RUMANIA

ETHIOPIA

FALKLAND ISLANDS

MONTSERRAT

GREECE

ANGOLA

RUMANIA

Stamps and music

For those interested in music, there are many interesting and colourful stamps covering all aspects of the subject. You can build up a good collection of stamps showing composers, instruments, scenes from operas and ballets and many other subjects of musical interest.

Our stamps show, first, a primitive type of bagpipe which is played in Rumania, followed by a Russian stamp showing a portrait of the famous composer Tchaikovsky. This is followed by one from Hungary, showing a circus clown playing all sorts of instruments, such as drums, a trumpet and cymbals.

The beautiful stamp from Venezuela is from a set devoted to various popular dances of that country. The stamp from Italy shows a portrait of the famous Italian conductor, Arturo Toscanini, and was issued in 1967 to mark the tenth anniversary of his death. The colourful stamp from the Togo republic in West Africa shows a native playing a drum and comes from a set devoted to the costumes and dances of that country. The final stamp, also from Hungary, shows a portrait of the famous composer and pianist, Franz Liszt. It also features a page of the music of one of his works and was issued in 1961 to mark the 150th anniversary of his birth.

These few stamps will give you an idea of the possibilities in this particular field of thematic collecting.

Music, musical instruments and musicians.

RUMANIA

RUSSIA

HUNGARY

VENEZUELA

TOGO

ITALY

HUNGARY

Stamps and paintings

Most of us cannot afford to own one of the world's great paintings. We can, however, make a very interesting gallery of our own through the medium of postage stamps.

Our first illustration is of a New Zealand Christmas stamp and shows 'The Holy Family' by the fifteenth-sixteenth century Italian artist, Titian. Next is illustrated a work, entitled 'The Messenger', by the twentieth-century French artist Georges Braque, and taken from the 1961 annual French set devoted to paintings. This is followed by a British stamp – 'Master Lambton' by Sir Thomas Lawrence, a great English painter, 'The Burgomaster' by Frans Hals, from the royal collection in Liechtenstein, 'Rooks have Arrived' by the Russian artist A. K. Savrasov, 'The Solitudes' by the Norwegian artist Edvard Munch and, finally, 'Breezing Up' by the American artist Winslow Homer.

Many beautiful stamps are also available which illustrate paintings from exotic countries such as China, Japan and India, as well as from the Middle East.

Great art and artists.

NEW ZEALAND

FRANCE

GREAT BRITAIN

LIECHTENSTEIN

RUSSIA

NORWAY

UNITED STATES

Stamps and literature

Most people enjoy reading books and seeing plays. Many writers of books and plays have been portrayed on stamps, as well as scenes from their works. Although the examples we have chosen refer mainly to people who wrote in the English language, writers in all languages have appeared on stamps.

The first two stamps come from Great Britain. The first was issued in 1966 and shows a portrait of the Scottish poet, Robert Burns. Russia, too, has issued a stamp in memory of Burns. The other stamp comes from a set issued by Great Britain in 1964, to celebrate the Shakespeare Festival. It shows Henry V praying in his tent on the eve of the battle of Agincourt. The Rumanian stamp was issued in 1960 and shows Daniel Defoe, who lived in the seventeenth-eighteenth centuries and wrote ' Robinson Crusoe'. The stamp from Eire (the Republic of Ireland) portrays the poet, W. B. Yeats.

Another stamp shown comes from Haiti, a small island in the West Indies. It shows the nineteenth-century French authors, Alexander Dumas, father and son. It was the father who wrote such works as 'The Count of Monte Cristo' and 'The Three Musketeers'. Finally, the American stamp shows Edgar Allan Poe, a poet and writer best known for his tales of mystery and imagination. It was issued in 1949.

Writers and poets.

GREAT BRITAIN

HAITI

RUMANIA

REPUBLIC OF IRELAND

UNITED STATES

Stamps about sports and pastimes

Ever since the revival of the Olympic Games in Athens in 1896, there has been no shortage of stamps illustrating every type of sport and pastime, whether it forms part of the Games or not.

The first stamp illustrated was issued by Great Britain in 1966 in connection with the World Cup. The stamp from Panama is interesting in that it shows underwater fishing. The French stamp is devoted to the much less strenuous activity of playing chess! Back to the more strenuous side, the Czech stamp features weight-lifting, while that from San Marino is concerned with mountaineering. The Russian stamp features hydroplaning, while the Rumanian stamp shows three patient fishermen waiting for a bite. Finally, the attractive stamp from Russia shows a line of people making their way up a gentle ski slope.

Once again, these stamps represent only a small selection of the many issues in this popular field.

Indoor and outdoor activities.

GREAT BRITAIN

PANAMA

FRANCE

CZECHOSLOVAKIA

SAN MARINO

RUSSIA

RUMANIA

RUSSIA

Stamps and space research

Man has been exploring space for a number of years, and it is interesting to follow his efforts by means of the numerous stamps on the subject of space exploration.

Naturally, most, but not all space stamps have been issued by the countries most actively taking part. Our selection has been made as wide as possible, both with regard to countries and subjects.

The first stamp from Poland shows a primitive rocket and a formula used in connection with it. The Bulgarian stamp was issued in 1963 after a Russian manned space-flight, while the second Polish stamp shows an example of a space-craft of the future amongst the various planets. The stamp from Togo shows Yuri Gagarin in his capsule in April, 1961. The Cuban stamp shows a very striking picture of a satellite encircling the earth and was issued in 1964. Finally, the stamp from North Vietnam was issued in 1961 when Major Titov took part in the second manned space-flight.

These are only a few of the very many stamps devoted to space research. This is now a very popular subject, particularly for young collectors.

Space-craft and space-men.

POLAND

BULGARIA

POLAND

TOGO

CUBA

NORTH VIETNAM

Stamps and alphabets

The so-called 'Roman alphabet' which we use, is also employed by a very large number of countries for writing their languages. However, there are many languages which use very different alphabets, and some which use none at all, employing other ways of putting their language in written or printed form. Examples of all these can be found on stamps, since most have printing on them. Our illustrations show a few typical examples.

The first stamp shows the alphabet used for writing Irish, while the next shows the two alphabets used in Yugoslavia – the Cyrillic and one similar to our own. The stamp from Monaco illustrates a variety of letters and syllables used in various world languages, while the Danish stamp has the words 'Red Cross' in many languages. The East German stamp shows the script that used to be employed for printing in German, while the Israeli stamp has the name of the country in English, Arabic and modern Hebrew. Finally, the stamp from Japan shows the syllabic characters used in Japanese writing.

Languages and alphabets.

REPUBLIC OF IRELAND

MONACO

YUGOSLAVIA

DENMARK

EAST GERMANY

ISRAEL

JAPAN

Stamps and maps

Maps of most countries and areas of the world have, over the years, appeared on postage stamps, so that it would be possible to compile a fairly complete atlas in this way. Our illustrations feature only a few examples.

It is appropriate that the Hungarian stamp should show a map of the world, since it was issued in 1957 to commemorate the seventieth anniversary of the world language, Esperanto. The Vatican City stamp shows the route of St. Paul's journey from Caesarea to Rome. The Austrian stamp is interesting in that it was issued to draw people's attention to the new system of postal areas into which the country is now divided. The next stamp, from the United States, shows a map of West Virginia. The stamp from Sharjah and Dependencies, the first to be issued by the territory in 1963, shows a map of these Trucial States on the Persian Gulf.

Finally, the stamp from Paraguay features a map of the solar system, showing the sun at its centre surrounded by various planets and showing their paths.

Maps of land and sky.

HUNGARY

VATICAN CITY

AUSTRIA

UNITED STATES

**SHARJAH
and Dependencies**

PARAGUAY

Stamps of peculiar shapes

The 'Penny Black' with its rectangular, almost square shape set the fashion for most stamps for many years – with one notable exception. This was the famous triangular stamp issued by the Cape of Good Hope as early as 1853. Our illustration shows a South African stamp issued in 1953 to mark the centenary of this Cape triangular stamp.

For a variety of reasons, triangular stamps have never proved very popular. However, they do appear from time to time, and our more modern second example comes from a set issued by Hungary in 1963. Diamond-shaped stamps also exist, and the example shown comes from Mongolia and was issued on the occasion of the World Cup in 1966. Two definite gimmicks in the way of peculiar shapes have been the stamps issued in 1964 by Sierra Leone, which were in the form of a map of the country and were also self-adhesive, and the circular stamps issued by Tonga in 1963-64.

Stamps of various shapes.

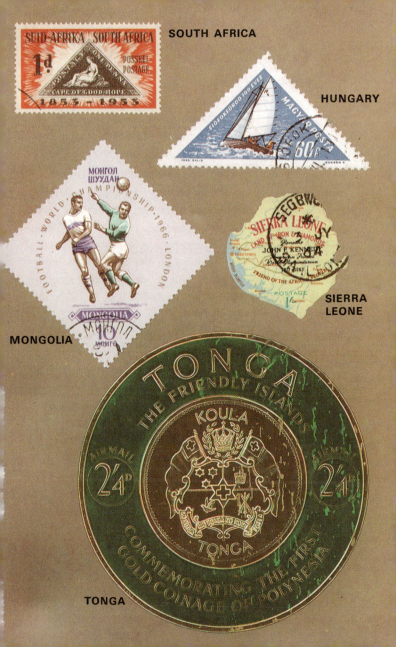

SOUTH AFRICA

HUNGARY

MONGOLIA

SIERRA LEONE

TONGA

Local and regional stamps

'Local' stamps may be described as those which, issued officially or privately, are restricted in use to a particular district, route or service. Many stamp catalogues do not list them, but they can be found quite often in stamp packets offered for sale. If you know what they are, they can be interesting additions to your collection.

One of our examples comes from Lundy, a privately owned island in the Bristol Channel. The owner first issued stamps in 1929 and they are valued in 'puffins', a puffin being equal to one penny, and the name being taken from that of a bird found on the island. The other local stamp is from Herm Island, one of the smaller Channel Islands. It was issued in memory of Sir Winston Churchill.

These 'locals' must not be confused with the 'regional' issues brought out by the British Post Office in 1958 for use in Jersey, Guernsey, the Isle of Man, Northern Ireland, Scotland, Wales and Monmouthshire. We have shown a selection of these. Note the tomato plant worked into the design of the Jersey stamp, and the Legs of Man (the Island badge) incorporated in the Isle of Man stamp.

Some local and regional stamps.

 **LUNDY**

 **HERM ISLAND**

 SCOTLAND

 ISLE OF MAN

 **GUERNSEY**

**WALES AND
MONMOUTHSHIRE** **N. IRELAND**

 JERSEY

Errors on stamps

Little or nothing that human beings make or do is perfect, and so we quite often find errors of various types in stamps. Some errors are very obvious, such as an aeroplane flying upside down and shown in the reproduction of a stamp issued in the United States in 1918. Other errors are so minute as to require a strong magnifying glass to detect them.

One of the most famous linguistic errors was on the French issue of 1937 to commemorate the 300th anniversary of the appearance of Descartes' book 'Discours de la Méthode'. At the first attempt the title appeared as 'Discours sur la Méthode'. It was later corrected. In a Greek issue of 1927 the name of an Englishman appeared first as 'Sir Codrington', later being corrected to 'Sir Edward Codrington'.

Other errors in designing have occurred at times, such as in the 1920 issue from St. Kitts-Nevis in which Columbus is seen looking through a telescope – though telescopes were not then invented!

Look carefully at your stamps and you, too, might discover some new errors.

Some obvious errors.

QU'AITI STATE IN HADHRAMAUT

FRANCE

GREECE

ST. KITTS-NEVIS

Curious stamps and stamps with a story

Stamp catalogues are full of interesting curiosities. The Russian stamp, printed on card in 1915, was used as a money voucher. During the periods of extreme inflation in Germany in 1923, and in Hungary in 1946, many stamps of seemingly very high face value were issued. However, they were not worth the paper they were printed on. The examples shown are of stamps supposedly worth five million marks and ten million pengös.

Because of a shortage of paper, the Latvian stamp (1920) was printed on paper intended for German bank notes. The very small stamp, having a value of two pfennig, had to be used on all letters posted within West Germany in 1948 in order to help with the rebuilding programme. The Greek stamp of 1954 shows an extract from the English parliamentary debates on the union of Cyprus with Greece – 'Enosis', deliberately disfigured by the Greeks with an ink blob.

A 'bisect' is a stamp cut in half, the two halves being used for half the original value. This happened in 1940, during the occupation of the Channel Islands by the Germans. 1d stamps were in short supply and authority was given by the Post Office for the use of British 2d stamps bisected diagonally. Two examples are illustrated.

Stamps of inflation, political propaganda and enemy occupation.

RUSSIA
Back of Stamp

HUNGARY

GERMANY

LATVIA
Back of Stamp

GREECE

WEST GERMANY

Forgeries, reprints, remainders and bogus stamps

Once stamp collecting developed into a profitable hobby and business, some dishonest people began to forge or make copies of rare and valuable stamps. The story of the work of some of these extremely clever forgers makes fascinating reading.

A 'reprint' is a stamp printed from the original plates after official issues have ceased. This is done for a variety of reasons, one of which is to meet the demand of collectors.

'Remainders' are stocks of old stamps which are put on the market by the issuing authority, often at a price below face value. This was recently done to a large extent by the Italian government.

Bogus stamps are not really stamps at all, but are issued for territories which do not exist. Our illustrations from South Moluccas (Maluku Selatan) in the East Indies, and the Principality of Thomond – supposedly in Ireland and issued in 1962–are examples of these. Collect them if you are interested, but realize that they are not really stamps.

Some bogus stamps.

SOUTH MOLUCCAS

THOMOND

Terms used in stamp collecting

As with most hobbies, there are many special terms used in stamp collecting. We have already mentioned some, and below are others you will frequently come across:

Block A group of not less than four stamps (not in a strip) still joined together as printed.

Cancellation A mark to show that a stamp has been used and to prevent re-use.

First Day Cover (F.D.C.) This is a cover bearing a stamp or stamps postmarked on the first day of issue. The G.P.O., and also other publishers, issue attractive First Day Covers, and an example is illustrated opposite.

Mint An unused stamp as originally sold and with full gum.

Overprint An addition; usually wording, printed on a stamp after its original production.

Postal Slogan This refers to wording such as 'Post Early for Christmas', etc., and is printed on envelopes, etc., by the cancelling machines.

Postal Stationery This refers to envelopes, postcards, etc., imprinted with a non-adhesive stamp. Air letters also come in this category.

Top: First Day Cover.
Centre: Postal slogans.
Bottom: Postal stationery.

GPO First Day Cover

20 FEB 1967
FIRST DAY OF ISSUE

Wills & Hepworth Ltd
Derby Square
Loughborough
Leicestershire

VISIT HISTORIC WARWICK IN THE HEART OF ENGLAND

EXMOUTH
SUNNY SOUTH DEVON
FOR HAPPY HOLIDAYS

WESTMINSTER ABBEY 900th ANNIVERSARY YEAR

BY AIR MAIL
PAR AVION
AIR LETTER
AEROGRAMME

NINEPENCE · POSTAGE

Terms used in stamp collecting (continued)

Roulette   Stamp separation by means of small cuts in the paper as distinct from the holes in normal perforation.

Se-tenant   This term is used when stamps of different design are joined together. This is deliberately done for producing some booklets of stamps but, in rare cases it can result from an error.

Strip   A single row of three or more stamps joined either horizontally or vertically.

Surcharge   An overprint to change the original face value of a stamp.

Tête-bêche   An inversion of one stamp in relation to the one joined to it — either vertical or horizontal.

Unused   A stamp that has not passed through the post but, because of its condition, is not fully mint.

Used   A stamp which is cancelled having done postal duty.

Variety   A stamp which shows differences from the normal design, paper, watermark, perforation or colour; not necessarily an error.

Stamp-collecting equipment

As with most other hobbies, there is a vast amount of equipment it is possible to use in stamp collecting. Very little of this is really essential, particularly for the general collector in the early stages.

However, you will need an album in which to stick your stamps. There are many types of these, ranging from those in which to keep specimens of stamps of the world, to those intended only for the stamps issued in connection with one special event. To start your collection, it is best to get an album covering the whole world, and in which the countries are arranged alphabetically or by continents. You must stick your stamps in the album with hinges, these being small pieces of thin paper gummed on one side, and which are folded over, one half being stuck to the album and the other to the stamp.

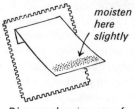

moisten here slightly

Diagram showing use of stamp hinges.

Use good quality hinges, as cheap ones can damage the stamps.

Other useful aids in collecting are an atlas to see where countries are, an encyclopaedia in which to find out more about what is shown on your stamps, a pair of tweezers and a magnifying glass.

You will need some form of reference book to help you classify your stamps according to country and date of issue. The various stamp catalogues meet this requirement. It is best if you first get a non-specialised catalogue covering all countries of the world, and in which most of the stamps are illustrated and priced according to mint (unused) and used copies. You will probably be able to borrow such a catalogue from your local public library or from a stamp club or society.

Obtaining stamps

Having obtained all your equipment, you will be wondering how to obtain stamps. There are many ways to do this.

You can go to your local dealer or, if you live in or near London, you will find numerous dealers in and around the Strand. You can also buy stamps – usually quite cheaply – at the auctions held by your local society or, if you are a more advanced collector, through your parents at public stamp auctions. Many people also buy stamps from the booklets in the packets which circulate amongst local society members, or those of other clubs and societies. It is possible to obtain approval sheets from dealers, these usually covering either cheap stamps or those of a more expensive type. Various commercial stamp firms also circulate boxes of low-priced stamps. You will find numerous advertisements about them in the various stamp magazines. If you find stamps in these boxes which are not in your catalogue, always ask an experienced dealer about them, as they may be bogus stamps.

Most towns or cities have a philatelic (stamp) club or society which will have both senior and junior members. If your town has one, do join it. You will meet collectors of all ages, hear talks about stamps and, what is perhaps most important, you will have a chance to see and examine all sorts of stamps. You will also have the benefit of the advice of older and more experienced members.

Most societies meet once a fortnight, and the subscription is usually quite low. Many have a library from which you can borrow catalogues, magazines and books about stamps, and also hold competitions which you can enter. Most schools have a stamp club: if yours does not have one, it would be a good idea to try to persuade one of the teachers to help you start one.